Raiment

Raiment

Marilyn Longstaff

Published 2010 by
Smokestack Books
PO Box 408, Middlesbrough TS5 6WA
e-mail : info@smokestack-books.co.uk
www.smokestack-books.co.uk

Raiment
Marilyn Longstaff
Copyright 2010 by Marilyn Longstaff
Cover image: *Marilyn and Tom, Redcar Beach* by John Longstaff
Author photograph by Pat Maycroft

Printed by
EPW Print & Design Ltd

ISBN 978-0-9564175-4-1
Smokestack Books gratefully
acknowledges the support of
Arts Council England

LOTTERY FUNDED

Smokestack Books is
represented by Inpress Ltd
www.inpressbooks.co.uk

Contents

'The life is more than meat, and the body is more than raiment.'
Luke 12:23

On Not Diving into the Wreck

She felt compelled to jump
although she knew even in
the heat of the day, this sea

was freezing, and that the currents
at the harbour mouth were worse than
treacherous.   She had a notion

that she would sink straight down, and yet
would still be able to see and breathe
as normal.   Needless to say

she didn't do it. Common sense
(where would she leave her handbag?)
and fear prevailed.   Instead

she sat basking in unexpected sun.
When she got home, she read
that poem by Adrienne Rich

about going down, down, down
confronting the wreck itself
which she herself had never done

although driving to see her friend Joanna
she had such good words in her head
good enough to release all that pain and anger.

Why didn't she write them down?

Vest

If anything
started it for me,
it was that string vest, or the ghost
of its diamond pattern
through semi-transparent nylon shirt
in a shade which wasn't mustard, it was paler,
but it was that sort of colour.

You must remember,
this was in the days before sex
on the telly. Mini skirts were just coming in,
but apart from a few tentative Levis and Wranglers
and the odd parka, the boys I knew still wore
grey flannel trousers and sports jackets
(with leather elbow patches).

I'm talking
of course, about where I lived
in a northern backwater, not Southend
or Brighton, with their invading mods
in smart suits, slim ties and fashionable
short-on-top, long-at-the-sides haircuts,
out for a day at the seaside on scooters.

Nothing much,
the hint of that vest
pulled taut against his shirt
next to his skin – as he played
table tennis at Darlington
Salvation Army youth club.
But it was a beginning.

ASH

I'd signed a pledge you see
so even flirting was not permitted,
but when my lover showed me
the rainbow colours of Russian Cocktail Sobranies
with gold tips,
and I ran my index finger along the smooth shank of a Camel,
breathed in the chaos of second-hand Gauloises,
I was tempted and I fell,
broke the vows and tasted long dark cigarillos.
I never learned the art,
never inhaled, never blew smoke rings,
gave it up before I started.

With age, I cursed the comrades in smoke-filled rooms,
campaigned for smoking bans in meetings,
while secretly admiring the stick-thin girls –
something to do with their hands,
the weight of silver rings, their bony fingers,
the elbow on the non-existent hip,
and the slight pause in their conversations
as they took a drag and turned their heads
to blow anonymous smoke signals.

Now, as I stand on Darlington's station
and read the notices
SMOKING FORBIDDEN
even at the extremities of the extremely long windswept platforms,
I'm thinking I'll take it up,
strike a light.

Indestructible Socks

Have you ever touched a pair
of *Indestructible Socks*?
They give you an electric shock
from triple thickness nylon static
in horrid colours. If washed in a
twin-tub, using the same water
left over from the whites,
they pick up all the bits of fluff,
and bobble. They never rot,
but go hard and discolour
at the heel and toe,
hold decades of foot odour
in their indestructible fibres.

What is there to say about men who wear
Indestructible Socks:
men of yellowing drip-dry shirts
and flowery kipper ties, loud
check jackets with armpit stains,
and flannel trousers;
teachers in sandals who don't care
enough about the kids
to make an effort. Who say,
'Take me as I am, or leave me.'

If forced into *Indestructible Socks*
I'd hide them under huge boots,
remove them at dead of night
in the bathroom, send them
to the launderette
with someone else's washing.

Blooding the Enemy

after Ian McDonald's photograph, 'Broken Nose'

The pig king has entered my classroom
late   as usual.
He's been fighting again.

And time stops as I drink him in,
savour his faint odour
of stale sweat/pigeon shit, under the Brut.

Outside the time-shift,
the rest smoulder –
ham-hand fingers fused into trotters,

solid-hunched, grunting –
these dark lords. I have nothing they want,
nothing to give them.

They know

it's my first year of teaching, know
I'm no Ursula Brangwen,
know

I didn't show who was boss
in the beginning – wearing those mini-skirts,
asking for trouble –

they smell my fear,
the fear of their victim,
and every week   they are waiting.

The pig king strolls to his desk,
stands, square-shouldered, to face me,
his lived-in jeans, zip straining,

shirt-sleeves rolled up to his biceps,
warrior's arms coated in bristle;
a small scar on his wedding-finger knuckle,

cruel stare FULL-ON, mouth so kissable,
daring me.
        'Why are you late? Where's your homework?'

He has my measure,
hands me a photo of himself at the door of his kingdom
'Fancy a visit   Miss?'

Tank Top

Knitting complex patterns in five colours
casts the blues away
I interwove a Fairisle tank top for my lover

In different colours, greens, I made a second for myself

I knocked a third one off, in purples, for my younger brother
who thanked me, loved it, threw it in the washer
reducing it to minute matted vest

I couldn't really say when I cast off my knitting

Hydroponicum Hot

Nature's World, Middlesbrough

Not hot like the tropical dome in the Eden Project
yet hot for our North-East climate;
hot compared with arctic uplands of Cow Green reservoir,

hot on this bench outside the hydroponicum
beside man-made lake, trickle of fountain.
Hot-breeze-rustle of willows, silver birches

muffles constant rush of Parkway traffic,
a cabbage-white kisses nameless flowers:
deep pink, rust orange, ragwort yellow.

My bare legs burn through Factor 15 lotion.
And I'm loving this – an unexpected pleasure.
I don't do happiness, but this comes close.

Illustrated Hymnal

Glad that I live am I
        gobstoppers and hard liquorice, sucked
        through a hanky, thinking Miss Feather won't notice
That the sky is blue
        steaming wellingtons too close to the coke stove
        and the smell of damp infants
Glad for the country lanes
        emptied galvanised bucket catches clanking raindrops,
        the school yard, an iron grey sea
And the fall of dew
        and sopping raincoats on the pegs
        and luke-warm milk with cod-liver oil capsules
After the sun the rain
        beyond the yard, hills of terraces –
        redbrick, their slates glistening
After the rain the sun
        wet playtime again and extra sums

This is the way of life
Till the work be done

All that we need to do
        is learn our letters and our tables,
        add up bakelite money, read 'Janet and John',
        avoid Miss Feather's ruler-edge on our knuckles
Be we low or high
        enough to look out of Victorian windows
        without standing on Miss Feather's desk,
Is to see that we grow
        like my Friday afternoon painting – a huge girl
        feet planted in emerald grass, triangle-skirted body
        in white no-man's-land, head in the clouds
Nearer the (bright blue) *sky.*

Postcard from Portivy

August 15th – a day for fêtes
picture us on the beautiful Côte Sauvage

we are tucking into local specialities
Moules Frites, Far Breton, and cheap ice-cold Muscadet

in generous plastic cups (forget tomorrow's headache)
sitting at street tables overlooking the harbour.

A few stalls selling day-glo sweets
and home-made jewellery. The weather is perfect.

Traffic banned, a mobile disco's in the Square
and everybody's dancing. Maybe it's a middle-aged thing

to be so delighted, as our kids remain unimpressed,
wanting to know what's happening next, but I don't think so.

French kids seem quite content with what's on offer.
So maybe it's the spoiled-brattedness of the English.

Whatever,   in a mix of squiffyness and exasperation,
after the umpteenth querulous *is this it then?* I respond

'What do you want, fireworks?'
They go home in a huff, back to the gîte to watch French
                                                       telly.

We stay, liberated, dancing, smiling – until the music stops
for an incomprehensible announcement.

All the street-lights dim, the crowd turns
towards a tiny offshore island for les feux d'artifice.

Looking for the Moon

Whenever a heavenly miracle is forecast
something not to be missed
can be witnessed only once in a lifetime

like the solar eclipse in August 2000

our weather on this awkward irascible island
puts the kibosh on it, *I'll show you*
don't think you can get excited.

The clouds join up, mist descends.
Might as well stay in bed – draw the curtains.
But on this night, conditions were perfect

to see an enormous low-rising moon,
so full and so close to Solstice
its like not seen for 300 years.

Somewhere around 11.30, when it got dark
we went out to walk the streets of Darlington
in search of the optical illusion.

You were hiding on the horizon

behind trees, offices, houses; nowhere
to be found. We dashed home, got in the car
drove in pursuit towards open countryside.

And then, we almost missed you –
sitting in the gap between hedges
half-way between Merrybent and Piercebridge.

Good job there was no traffic.
You brought us to a dead halt
with your attitude, your foreignness.

A butter globe of hope and happiness.
We laughed at our ridiculous midnight.
And we were glad of it.

22 June 2005

Valentine's Day Walk in Wensleydale

Shift clouds,
sky-blue-pink
to *Quink*.

Negotiating bog
and ford, we land
below high Stalling Busk, to stand

mother and daughter,
in the shadow of unsafe ruined church,
by rarely ruffled Semerwater.

In the redundant graveyard
where weathered stones and
scrappy trees lean,

shock of the new hard
dark marble,
'Both sometimes of High Blean'

in the same incongruous grave
father and son lie
a month between.

Sheets of hail twist and wind;
untethered shrouds
lashing our cheeks red raw.

Un-named Spring

A ford, marked on the map –
in wet February, at this same spot, a torrent,
causing him to search for a crossing place upstream,

but now, all that can be heard
is the trickle of slow water underground.

A tiny trout, trapped in a rock pool which had seeped away,
its comma curl flat on dry limestone page.
Like the china carp in Bowes Museum,
caught, proud of its glazed oval pond dish.

Death pursues him in the form of stranded creatures,
the fish in the trainer on St Ives beach,
the foul rabbit soup with Ivan Denisovich eye
that poured from a fallen hollow road-post he picked up
at the side of Beggarman's Road. And now this.

In a month's time, a fat baby blackbird will fly
straight at the kitchen window as his mother washes up

and drop like a stone.

Heron

Uncomfortable in his shape, he hated
the weight of himself, that he could break
her wrist with an affectionate squeeze.

But height was his real burden. He walked
with his head hunched into his neck, to try
to make himself look shorter.

All this did was draw attention to his legs.
Is the air a bit thin up there? complete strangers
would joke; couldn't fathom why he didn't find this funny.

Always, he tried to hide his size 16 feet,
under a chair, behind a table. Paddling
was good – he could sink a few inches.

He sweated a lot. A fine sheen
on his brow made him look varnished.
No-one knew where he'd come from –

an oval peg in a round hole – his Dad
was five foot four, his Mum smaller. He was taller
than his brothers, school friends, work mates –

head and shoulders. He wore a lot of grey
to try to blend into the background.
Asked himself, often, what she saw in him.

The Language of Silk Knickers

The time he started to buy her the silk knickers
was the time she started to give up on him.

Everything sealed, kept in his head, broke out
in those little packets that weighed nothing:

One black pair with frilly sides,
the other, lace-fronted ivory.

She'd always had nice hair, bright eyes,
neat tits, malleable lips, but

her bum had never been her best feature,
not pert, even in her prime. Someone she knew,

once called her *Thunder Thighs*.
The knickers felt nice, looked ridiculous,

like Dame Edna in a tutu, or the Archbishop
of Canterbury in shorts.

The ivory ones too tight, the black
made her skin look pale and pimply;

neither were machine washable,
or returnable.

Ken and Deirdre Dreaming

Ken Barlow is sitting up in the double bed.
He is on the right hand side as I look at it.
He is wearing uncreased, buttoned, tartan pyjamas.
His hair is immaculate, shades of blonde/grey.
His glasses – half moon – are perched towards the end
of his nose. His knees are raised under the bed-clothes.
He is attempting yesterday's *Guardian* crossword.

Deirdre has flung her side of the covers off
lying diagonally   her feet in the space
where Ken's would be if he stretched his legs
her arms sprawl this way and that
face down   she's chucked the pillows
naked except for specs   and that enormous
snake tattoo   red black and blue   writhing
from left shoulder to right buttock

The Joke

Yes, we were in a bar.

No it wasn't very far from here;
might have been *The Turks Head*
before it was themed. No, I'm wrong
it was the old *Kings Arms*. Must be
at least twenty years since they demolished it.

We'd gone there after a Labour Party meeting.
Needed to calm down. There'd been a big row,
between the 'our lads need the jobs' faction
and the 'save the environment' lobby,
over plans to sink another potash mine

just outside Whitby. John got the beers.
The pub was rowdy – juke-box playing
'Stand By Your Man', and the half-pissed
members of the *Caged Birds Society*
(+ birds) were joining in.

I hear better with a bit of background noise
(funny that; no-one believes me)
so I think I was the only one who caught
Gerry's story (he's dead now, of course).
Trouble is, I've never been too good at listening.

Yes, there might have been a gorilla in it.

In Praise of My £3 White Plastic Alarm Clock

Thankyou
for your insistent triple-bleep repeat that pierces
the invisible cotton wool of my deafness
and rescues me
to drink still warm-enough bedside tea which lubricates
my snore-dry mouth

drags me from nightmare-sleep – that panic dream again
of rushing to catch an impossible train,
the only one to Ipswich, a place
I'm not sure why it's imperative for me to reach.

I glimpse an old red double-decker
pull away.
The capped conductor winks
and mouths, 'Ipswich', as he yanks the cord to ring the bell.

There are three of us.
One has disappeared to make train enquiries.
The other turns on me
and I'm thrown naked – did I mention that?
(apart from a towel that keeps slipping)
into the back of a speaking van.

It is beyond dark and I am groping to find my knickers
in the detritus of plastic bags which contain the haste of our leaving.
Shall I just abandon them and pull on the skin-tight
pale-blue satin-textured drainpipe jeans and sockless black stiletto boots?

I think so.
I'm writhing like a snake on LSD to shrug off
this orgasmic ache
and it's not working.

Don't you just feel that – if you could breathe through your nose
if you didn't eat nuts just before bedtime
if hot flushes didn't drown you and your knees just didn't ache
if you could sort out just what you were doing and where you were going,
                    you could banish these dreams to the recesses
                    of abandoned underground stations,

but you still have the travelling itch,
third class – and no destination
except, perhaps,   Ipswich.

Lost for Words

I'm sitting in an inadequately organised oblong seminar,
so every time our tutor turns his head from left to right,
I can catch only the half of what he's saying.

It's like *Singing in the Rain*,
when the silent movie star can't get used to the microphone.
Then my battery dies

and the little I could hear dies with it.
Can I find the replacement?
Not until all the contents of my handbag

have been sifted at least twice.
Struggling to insert-new-battery-in-hearing-aid-under-table,
I'm missing everything.

I want to say, *For Christ's sake SPEAK UP*
but I'm sick of making that request
and I don't do blasphemy.

At last, I insert the functioning beige eartrumpet
just in time for 15 minutes silent scribbling.
Now, I can hear

        rustling of felt tips on paper,
        gurgles of swigging water,
        deafening throat clearing.

Middle-aged Woman Writes about a Houseplant

From long exposure to the direct sun
her houseplant leaves
took on the look of bacon – overdone.

And she liked that look;
complemented her overcooked egg plant
        which hath not born fruit,
her shrivelled tomato,
        which she had neither watered nor fed,
the limp mushrooms under her sink,
        that she had planted not, nor yet asked to grow.

And she liked the thought
of this overcooked
inedible vegetable-matter version
of a carnivore's Full English Breakfast,
dried up and withered like her love
for the overdone man
who'd given her the houseplant

and liked his meals just like that.

Posing in Front of the Hashish Store, 1978

What gave me away?
the mem sahib bit in Darra,
cotton sun hat
and although I'm wearing Afghan
ankle-tight blue drawstring trousers,
bought in a Kabul bazaar –
posing in front of The Hashish Store –
I still look like a missionary
or an English Sunday School teacher.

Maybe it was
the bottle of Rose's Lime Juice
in the New Delhi YMCA,
that rucksack full of Andrex toilet paper
or the Tupperware box of medical equipment
for every conceivable complaint
except being hit by a stray bullet
from a hand gun, fashioned like a pen,
made in the single socket factory
in this frontier town.

Postcard from Languedoc

Day 3 – it's pissing down,
chats et chiens,
and I'm wearing a vest,
a shirt, two cardigans,
warm trousers, thick socks,
a scarf, my anorak,
and carrying Mum's flowery parapluie,
to take this card – of sun-soaked
vineyards, and boats on the *Canal du Midi* –
to the post. Guess I'll be home
before you get this. Love Me.

Hairy Story

Imagine Rapunzel bald.
No amount of sitting in the ivory tower
and wishing for her prince to come
will bring about release.
She contemplates her fate:

even if he could climb the ivy,
use crampons and other mountaineering tools,
abseil from the castellated roof,
swing from a helicopter wire,
hire a microlight
have himself catapulted from a trebuchet,
become a human cannonball,
trampoline, pole vault,
walk a tightrope from a neighbouring turret…

She has had time to plait
endless possibilities for fairy story rescue, but
she looks into her glass –
even if
he should penetrate all defences,
effect entry, what would he find –
a maiden without her crowning glory.
Thanks, but no thanks, I'll pass.

The future's looking grim. Time
to turn to faith and prayer,
promise anything in return for hair.
She specifies, *thick yet fine,*
fine, thick, black hair,
silky, black, thick, fine hair;
she repeats this mantra from under her mantilla,

pledges eternal platitudes,
this is all she wants, all she will ever ask for,
she will never, never ask for anything
again, just this one thing

to make her dreams come true. Then
one night it

starts
        fast and thick
        thick and black
        black and fine
        fine and silky
        silky, black, thick, fine hair

sprouts
        from her thighs to her toes,
        from her upper lip
        from her armpits to her fingertips

grows and grows and grows and grows and grows;
first long enough for a light permanent wave,
then bunches, a ponytail, then
long plaits which trail from her
prison window, down down
to the ground and further.

Bald-pated Rapunzel
sits at her leaded casement
recalling Midas' disaster
knows she's got
exactly what she asked for.

Serpent Farmhouse

High on the hills above Healaugh
you are skulking in shadow
like a Chinese Dragon redundant
after New Year celebrations.
Your path-tail snakes behind
and you've sunk your fangs
deep into bedrock.

Two white door eyes are watchful.
I feel them on my back
as I'm snaking up
the abandoned lead-mine hush
on the dark side of the valley.

The sky is moving fast. The sun's
rushing across the fell-side.
Serpent beware,
its light will soon expose
your buried intentions.

Dream Cottage

Our dream cottage, whitewashed cobbles – breaking down –
home-made mortar reducing to original mix – sand, saltwater –

The house is crying.
It has the smell of crypts.

Where we lean against bedroom wallpaper
our backs are wet.

We are cowering here, escaping the kitchen.
The warm moist air has brought them out.

They are thin and straight and black as 4B pencils,
they don't wriggle or squirm,

but move in silent lines across the linoleum
to disappear under the ancient enamel gas cooker.

Down at the harbour
old fishermen are creating model villages from beach pebbles.

It Never Felt Like This

after Tracey Emin

'off with those shoes,' John Donne

In red ankle-strap stilettos,
the type I never wore, even before bunions,
I'm bending over my Edwardian bath

(in need of enamelling)

remembering that conversation
about how we would undress,
and what would be the last to go –

for you it was your socks.

Next to naked,
I fiddle with original brass taps,
sweal away tidemarks.

This bath takes an age to empty.

IT NEVER FELT LIKE THIS

when I had shoulder-length hair
and thin thighs,
when my stomach didn't roll against the roll-top.

You swore you loved me. *YES YOU DID.*

AND YOU KNEW you were lying.
And I know I am slipping, sliding
on the wet floor of memory, your last fall

from ice waterfall in your 38th February.

AND YOU KNEW IT WOULD FEEL LIKE HELL.
And it feels like hell,
twenty years on.

On the Occasion of Her Greatest Disappointment (to date)

This one she can't hide, behind the fire-screen
in her over-furnished pleasant dwelling.

This one is not like her irritating bedroom carpet which
she conceals under fine Indian rug. It will not disappear.

Soon, the punters will be swarming in for the auction preview to
uncover

her chest-of drawers is not solid dovetailed pine with firm handles,
sale-room wardrobe – veneer peeling in over-hot central heating –
not a bargain,

her bedrock is not strong – its fault-lines are creaking,
outlook to front and rear displeasing.

Here, for once, she thought she had found
something she was at ease with.

And she allowed herself to hope (mistake),
and make this hope public (mistake).

How was she to know that the salesmen were disingenuous?

And she discovers that she has been sold
an un-named pup she never wanted

that widdles on her floors, leaves dog-hairs on her pillow,
chews at the soles of her most comfortable slippers.

And although she has burnt its basket,
rationed its daily dose of Chappie,

spoken to it harshly, wagged her finger,
nothing has worked.

She feels she may have no alternative but to see it painlessly
destroyed.

Walking Someone Else's Dog

for Holly

The way she carried it in her mouth, half-dead;
her sulky refusal to give it up, the look she gave me.

The way she tortured the blind scrap, then wolfed it down,
missing a ruby fragment that lay on the ground.

The way she went back to the hole she had dug out
to get the other; how I got her to drop it, barely living,

its eyes not yet open. How I covered it up with my foot
in earth, its nest broken, buried alive to salve my conscience,

its black silk fur, its pink hand curled on its chest.

Next of Kin

I was asked for my next of kin, 'Just a formality
if anything happens on the hike.' I made up Mike,
Mike Nicholls, 14, Spring Gardens, Hetheringstall,
M33 4ZU. I said he was my brother.

I hope no-one has to contact him. Mike's very shy.
He's asked me not to put him down on forms, but
I've no other alibi. He's 6ft 2 and blond, wears glasses
has a squint. His hair is thinning now

just at the temples. He works in a department store
in Oldham. Never married; had a girlfriend once,
called Sandra. She ditched him for a merchant seaman.
Mike lived with Mum until she died.

Stayed on in the bungalow – it seemed easy.
He'll be 52 next birthday, January 5th. If I go first,
which seems quite likely, I'll leave him
all my worldly goods – they don't amount to much:

a few bun pennies, my clothes, *Love Me Do*
by the Beatles, some sticks of furniture. I travel light.
What more could he ask from me?
I've given him a life.

Figment

Fragment found in the Bodleian Library, Oxford, between the pages of Newton's Principia Mathematica

My stuffed-shirt arm weighs heavy on this paper.
My desk draws me here, folds me into the pages,
chains me in the vellum shelves.

I hold my pen and I dip it in the ink.
All I write is this, 'Dearest,
Mrs. Jenkin's guest-house porridge lies like millstone grit in my
        stomach'.

I want to write,
'My love, yellow and green light shards
stab at the gulf between us.

I think of you in that grey blue waste,
the empty space that strings Craster, Bamburgh, Berwick
the thin line we walked between sea and sand....'

24th August 1919

You

There you are in the military-green hospital wrap,
a red head screaming at the interruption of being born;

shock of hazel eyes and sad mouth in the playgroup portrait,
silver-sand hair cut in a mullet by the child-minder's children;

saucer-smiling in front of the half-demolished shed,
in your Dad's old rolled-up cords and size 8 boots.

A child who didn't want to read and loved running.
I'm late and worrying I won't recognise you –

although I know you better than I know myself,
I know you not at all. Ridiculous – of course it's you,

your tall assurance, easy style in *Topman* faded denim,
stripy top and flip flops – in Winter,

and your open grin as you give me a hug, say 'Oh my God,
I've just got some men's white linen trousers

and had to try them on in the men's changing rooms.'
I speculate about how we've both been mistaken for men

with our broad shoulders, narrow chests, long legs, confidence,
as you talk about things I'll never comprehend

and drink banana milk shake with cooked dinner,
in *Café Neon*.

Les Pérseïdes

Imagine walking a coast path
marked *Sentier* –
the tide has turned
and is seeping away.
Moored boats
lean into muddy dreams
while a fresh water channel
shrugs free from its sea blanket.
Oyster beds, water tanks, small wrecks,
rub away sleepfulness.
Ignore the diversion inland,
trespass by derelict outbuildings,
into twilight.
Then you come upon it –
a long long whitewashed
single-storey lean-to
(in England
it would be straight out of Dickens)
windows, all facing out
across Plouharnel Bay
to campsite lights
on the Quiberon peninsula.

We were expected –
Luc, Roman, Danni and Philippe
were waiting to greet us
welcomed us into
white painted wood-lined interior
and loaded dining table –
plateau de fruits de mer –
a leisurely feast
and lots of laughter.
And after, into the bright dark
we went outside for coffee,
drank Breton apple *digestif*,
lay back in patio chairs,
feet up on a makeshift table
to contemplate the Milky Way,
Scorpio, the Plough *(comme une casserole)*,
waited, waited
with wide-eyed concentration
for fleeting fire-tails
silent dust from comets.

13 August 2004

After the Tympanoplasty

Yesterday, for the first time
since-I-don't-know-when,
I didn't wear a hearing aid.

Could just about hear
the bedroom clock ticking, John talking,
watch TV with the volume lower.

Walking into town, I found
I quite liked the music in T.K.Maxx,
felt 10 years younger, wanted to dance.

Can still hear the clock and the noise of traffic;
it is Winter and we have seen no sign of snow,
here in the deep North-East.

After a week of heavy frosts and china-blue skies,
we hear it's coming – rumours of flurries nearer the coast,
in Whitley Bay and Tynemouth.

We know it's been blessing the Highlands,
but the thick knee bandage on last night's weather map
leaves this northern thigh naked.

Today the sky has turned grey.
As the glacier in my right ear allows a crevasse of hearing,
others are waking to that cold cotton-wool deafness.

Please Use Style

hammered in an ancient metal sign
on a rusting and collapsing iron gate
near the top of Wether Fell by Yorburgh,

the sun fighting a losing battle with low freezing mist
and me doing the same with frozen snowdrifts.

I try to please, consider my walking kit –

sturdy brown sensible boots
(replacements for malachite green but worn-out beauties)
workmanlike navy cotton trousers, essential walking pole.

But my anorak's amethyst with a lemon flash,
my gloves lavender,
my stripy Dennis the Menace charcoal and ruby wool hat
with soft redcurrant fleece lining, an Angela Bradley original.

Then there's my good Shetland jumper in blueberry,
aubergine, banana, orange, emerald and fuchsia.
Ah yes, and the mint linen shirt,

and Italian polka dot
silk knickers with a hint of lace –

as I stylishly squeeze through the broken gate.

Pilgrimage

for Jackie

Beyond the false calm of Muker car park and
Level paths across set-aside meadows –
Indulgent lying-in, under snow blankets – we reach
Zs of the River Swale in blast valley,
Zero tolerance for fools who've ventured out.
Angry landscape, it lashes us, unleashes furious
Rods of iced-venom, funnelled and shot
Down this tunnel of doom.

Silent and intrepid, we press on towards Kisdon.
No shelter
Our heads lowered to shield cheeks from
Weather beating. The gale is
Shouting, but we are deaf in our stupidity,
Neither willing to be the first to give in.
Oligarchs of the State of Stubbornness,
We press on. A man with dog

Stumbles out of the white-out,
Laughs, 'It's wild in there.'
Extreme cold.
Extreme wet.
The full force of 'March wind doth blow'

Straight at us.
No shelter, no turning back, with
Only the possibility of sandwiches to sustain us,
We press on.

As we climb past abandoned lead mine,
Reach the top, the clouds lift
And the sun seduces my packed lunch,
Your flask, from sodden rucksacks.
Only one bite, one sip, be-
Fore you glance behind.

So, that was that then. Purple
Night is racing towards us again. Break
Over, food thrown back into packs,
We press on through blizzard and
Dee ee eep drifts, down, down to cross the falls.
Rushing, we lose the way. On the far bank,
Inch up treacherous snow and ice cliff,
Floundering,
Thigh deep, but determined we won't turn back. We

Struggle to high path and dry interval,
Lounge on a tree-trunk-seat for delayed snack.
It's decision time – the sky track,
Ploughing into cloud, or the
Safer route? We go for the
Lower. On the home stretch now, we wind
In and out of snow pockets on this
Dark side that holds no homesteads,
Each relieved to have reached the

Turn, we wallow in hallucinations of dry feet,
Escapist dreams of mythical tea rooms
And crackling fires, honey; we need to
Run as it grows yet darker,
Or we'll miss this chintz antithesis.
On our knees like pilgrims, we
Make it – last orders for tea and scones.

Corridor Photographs: Ward 14

Canal

Trees line either side, then rows upon rows
stretch behind to the vanishing point. The trees
are tall and slim, tall and slim. There are no leaves.

The light is a grey light, dawn – twilight?
There is no snow, yet it feels like Winter,
appears silent. Trunks and branches

reflect in both sides of the silver water
black arms and bony fingers that never meet.
They leave a burnished silver channel

beaten with reflected rain clouds.
The canal curves to narrow in the distance.
Outside Ward 14

an April tree waves its new green feathers.
Through open-slide grey-tinted hospital window
a defiant strip is bright with Spring sunshine.

At this height I can see
TV aerials, slate roofs, brick chimneys,
my Crescent sharp-curved at its cusp,

but I'm in this hothouse prison, for the time being.

Pond

Trees in a clump
by the edge of round foreground water
rise to a mid point. It is still Winter.
Intense light stares to beam a path
across the pond's surface.
I could step out of this corridor
into this silver frame, tread
that shining path. Be free

of the padded walk of hospital
professionals, jar of lavatory door
clatter and *What would you like
darling?* of the tea trolley
smell of microwaved dinners
slap of rubber sheets, creak
of crutches.
When can I go home?

Settling

The ginger cat who goes with me
rotten with fleas, was dragged
spitting and howling, doused
in clouds of choking white powder; de-loused –
adopted by The Evangelical Christian Family
to be rescued from the perdition of a wicked nature.

I am Felix. I'll go along with it. Purr
on their cushioned rocking chair
nearest the fire – permit
some stroking. It's comfortable
for the time being, until they threaten
neuter.

I'm off, hitching a lift on the back of
a university. Death of God,
the unsheathed claws of philosophy.
But homing instinct
draws me back again and again,
so although I walk the fence, shit
in flowerbeds, worry the odd tit,
truth is, I've settled for something.

Outsider

Six hundred thousand live in this city
wear the starred armband, walk in the gutter
help build the walls that seal their ghetto.

Inside the wire, ice-thistle skeletons;
jack-booted lights selecting at random –
bullet in the head for the girl who asks the question

'Where are we going?'

I'm walking a footpath just outside this tableau
in the bottom right-hand corner of the valley of the shadow
– a long way to climb to that solitary tree's glow

far far beyond my small horizon.

The Wreck

They are sitting in the plane-spotters' lay-by
in a white bottom-of-the-range hatchback, new
when the affair started, now covered in rust
and well past its sell-by-date.

                              It is her car.
She's in the driving seat. Rigid and
looking out of the windscreen, she sees him
in her driver's mirror, his skin the colour
of albino shit; the starch has gone out of him.
She can see his lips working
and he is muttering rubbish
as he hands her back her k.d. lang CDs
Don't take this the wrong way; I need
to draw a line under it.

The Language of Surgeons

if I ram
   ram the broo

        broom handle up
           up his refined arse

shove his refined head
      head into a bucket

          bucket of his own piss
            shit/piss

hold the stinking revolver
  to his stinking blindfold

play one-doctor Russian Roulette until I
blow his stinking brains out

burn the shitty body   clean up
   the stinking mess

shower
put on my concert dress

go to Schubert's String Quartet
repeat   repeat   repeat

time and a
     time and again

will I have buried him dead
will my purified tongue rise from
     his refined ashes

That Dream Again

The shoes were there –
one black, one white,
just like at university
when me and Helen swapped one each
to see if our philosophy professor
would notice
in the *Problem of Evil* seminar.

Surprisingly he did.
Commented on mine as
interesting. I said,
'Helen has a pair just the same.
Look.' He raised his left eyebrow
and continued with Karl Barth
(or it might have been Leibniz).

But the dream shoes were not like those –
not like the clompy shoes I wear.
These were pointed-toed stilettos.
Trouble was, the heels
were different heights, so when I walked,
I was the visual equivalent
of Eeyore's voice – up and down,
up and down – unsteady.

Then you appeared,
recurred like a bad dream,
which, of course, you were – are,
bobbing about too,
somewhere behind me,
like one of those nodding dogs
on a saloon car parcel shelf.
I think you were hovering
above my right shoulder.

What's good about all this
is that I found you a bit weedy,
a bit pathetic, a bit of a nuisance;
not in the least attractive. What's bad
is that you're still pestering me.
                    And I am hamstrung,
limping a half-life
unable to move on.

Maybe, the hobbled black and white shoes
will rescue me,
in some kind of hop-along fashion.

Bedtime Stories

Fresh in her clean cotton nightie
tucked in between tight crisp sheets
under scratchy blankets, her father
in his slippers sitting on the chair
beside her bed recounting stories
from his childhood. And she doesn't
know what to do. He always tells her
something for a reason. He is looking
straight ahead into the distance.

*

The imagined sound
of her father as a boy –
a different sort of creature,
before he gave his heart to
Jesus – bringing the snails
into the kitchen in his
trouser pocket, placing
them slowly, one by one,
onto the hotplate, leaving
enough time between to
hear each sizzle and scream,
to inhale the stench.

*

Another view of her father –
that he could be cruel for pleasure,
a sense of his confession,
a warning against her own nature,
how 'man' is sinful and needs
redeeming grace.

*

And later, I am cruel
to my friend's younger sister
making her cry and finding it funny
and the afterwards horror

and the comfort of repentance.
And my adult rejection of magic solutions

and the recognition that salvation
is in my own hands; which is scary.

Agent for the Lord

My dad is Vladimir Putin and Daniel Craig
(James Bond) rolled into one,
with his steel eyes, hairless torso,
cheese-wire lips, and nose bent like a crowbar.

Brigadier Crowhurst, agent for The Lord,

is on a mission,
flicks a speck of dust from his uniform cap,
examines the browning celluloid interior,
presses his own trousers under a damp tea-towel.

Undercover agent for The Master,
the cap's peak shadows his brow,
casts a slant to his thin mouth,
keeps the lid on his sinful nature.

Inscrutable.

His deadly weapons, sword and shield
a bow of burning gold,
arrows to pierce Satan's armour –
he sees Satan everywhere.

Checking his Trinity watch, it's time
to mesmerize his captive audience with The Story,
let them know he has a hot-line to the man-in-charge
who promises promotion,   glory.

In Praise of My Father, Salvation Army Officer and Cobbler of Renown

Sundays, he's never in his cobbling shed,
up at dawn to turn the Citadel heating on,

hangs up his apron, dons his uniform
for a full day's hot evangelistic zeal.

Brass band and chatty congregation,
seamed-stockinged Songsters rustle

as they kneel.

        Clank of iron last
and hammering in of segs and blakies,

he cobbles my unredeemable high heels
in the shed he's built from old mahogany wardrobes,

his calloused hands ingrained from dirty labours,
rendered unclean for preaching, praying,

comforting the sick. He's more at home
with the tube of strong black glue he uses

for fixing rubber soles.

Keeping Up

Dad
every night
polished our shabby
shoes   to high shine
If we could have afforded
fancy knickers, they would have bathed
in reflected glory on mirrored toe caps

Slingbacks

Shuffling in slingbacks
the slingbacks   so slung back
your foot slips out and you have to walk
without lifting your feet from the ground
and scuff

I can hear Dad shouting
PICK YOUR FEET UP

Gluttony

Ferragamo, Christian Dior, Chanel,
Givenchy, even though they were pinchy,
shiny high heels, strappy pumps, boots, sandals,
soft leather moccasins, the black canvas
espadrilles she wore when she fled to Hawaii
made locally, in Marikina city.

Imelda Marcos got extremely cross
at press reports that she had 3,000
pairs of shoes. *They went into my closets*
looking for skeletons, but all they found
thank God, were shoes, beautiful shoes.
I had 1,570.
Everybody kept their shoes there. The maids…
everybody. They were all size 8 and a half.

Fuck-me-shoes

for Germaine Greer and Jimmy Choo

Purposeful soft leather lace-up in American Tan
or
silver kitten heel with a hint of fuchsia feather for an upper
you know are not for walking

Choose fuck-me shoes
Go on
you know you want to...

Cornish Pasty Shoes

Could you ever fancy a man
in Cornish Pasty shoes?
The sort that has one seam off centre
on the upper and crimps round
to emphasise his big toe.

I know I couldn't. Where's the symmetry?
Where would his nose, eyes, mouth, balls be?
Would he have one arm, one leg, one ear –
all on one side of his body?

Leopard Skin Stilettos (size 7)

impossibly high
tight-lipped winklepickers hide
retractable claws

Apathy or disgust?

horrid white slip-ons with gold chains (for men)
even worse with a bit of a cuban
heel, and pink socks, both in size 11
the sort suave men without style put on
with not-quite-long-enough *sta-prest* trousers

not sure what emotion this arouses
not envy, anger, covetousness, lust

Last Words to My Mother

What might the last words be for
                    a wordsmith
                    an aficionado of cross words
                    a Bible thumping preacher
                    a human pre-computer spell-checker
                    a nit-picking corrector of bad language
                                and bad grammar?

Yes, this man was my father.

And his last words
'How about a game of Scrabble?'

Message from the Dead

A birthday card from Dad
was in the clearance pile, some rural scene
bought from the V & A.

I must have kept it for its rarity.
Mum did cards, except for Valentines
when I bought Dad's for her.

At first, I hadn't recognised
the name – thought it said Fred
(Dad's writing was appalling) –

until I got it into daylight.
Felt sad that he had died so long ago
even his writing had become a blur,

from Dad with all good wishes
on your birthday, and the message
in another colour, *Prov. 3. (5-8)*

Now more than 30 years have passed
he's sending me a text,
as I'm grieving in my small and quiet way
for Julia Darling, who I knew a little:

Trust in the Lord with all thine heart:
and lean not unto thine own understanding.
In all thy ways acknowledge him,
and he shall direct thy paths.
Be not wise in thine own eyes;
fear the Lord and depart from evil.
It shall be health to thy navel,
and marrow to thy bones.

15 April 2005

Raiment

The church is sunny on this
November Saturday morning
as more than 700 meet
to say goodbye to Marjorie.

Altar boys with military haircuts
in white gowns and sharp red trainers
take their duties seriously. Incense swings,
bells dong intermittently.

Seven priests dispense wine and wafers.
There will be serious alcohol later.
My first Catholic funeral.
A strange journey for a post-Christian

Salvationist. The choir and congregation
sing at half the speed I'm used to,
Thine be the glory. There is no Band
to hurry things along, no Songsters.

Priests, pallbearers, chief mourners
slow-march towards the front door.
The waiting hearse whisks the coffin
to Sunderland for cremation.

No *angels in bright raiment* here,
no stone will be rolled away –
only a wake at the social club,
loved-ones raising a few glasses.

On the Mappa Mundi

Mixed up among accurate cities and rivers,
the naked monopod on his back, solitary
leg in the air, using his giant foot as umbrella –
factual accounts of fish-men caught in nets
and shining men coming down from the sky.

And somewhere on this map, and in other
records, on the edges of the known, a race
of dog-head men, although no mention of
bitch-head women, like men in every detail
(eating the same food, living in villages,
and wearing the same raiment)   save one.

And what exercised The Church? Not the question
of their existence, but *Do these creatures have a soul?*
Have some adopted Christianity? And so it carries on.

No Faith

Trapped in an air-conditioned windowless seminar on a lovely day
being preached at by a humanist Star Trek fanatic from the BHA
I have Star Trek – every single episode on DVD.
Fantastic. Let's worship at the shrine of Gene Somethingorother,
its humanist creator.

He starts with the symbol of the happy human, outlines the
                                        secularists' hagiography:
as Epicurus (a signed up member of the British Humanist
                                        Association)
said – in Greek – "friendship goes dancing all around the world
encouraging us to a happy life" (nothing wrong with HEDONISM).

I lose the will….,
come round at EM Forster, or was it Aldous Huxley,
who *had a very long-term satisfying relationship with another man*
                                        in Cairo,
name of Muhammad,
                and he was a bus conductor.

And I am
hot-eyed in a desert sandstorm, with conjunctivitis and a leaking
                                        meiobian cist

squeezing my feet back into my shoes at the end of a 24 hour coach
trip to Barcelona when the temperature has risen by 20° C

forced into man-made, polyester, short-crotch tight-waist pyjamas

deafened by a high-pitched continuous siren at full volume in close
                                proximity to the twin hearing aids

bedazzled by red and green stripes in a Bridget Riley painting   .

gagging at a combination of trifle and tripe with a slice of andouille
on my tongue

                        and I CAN'T SWALLOW IT

Today

I shall go out today alone
down, down through the pine forest
down to the river I have heard of.

No-one will see me
from their shuttered rooms.

I'll loosen my waist
unleash my hair
wear a black cotton dress
from my secret stash.

I'll look for the sun
see what colour the sky is
listen for un-named birds
that are not owls or nightjars.

I shall not take my fan
or sal volatile.
I'll talk all day about reds
and blues and yellows,

roll in river mud
wriggle my toes in pine needles.
If I want, I'll frown, though
a half-smile might play

at the corners of my mouth
as I imagine the absurdity
of Arthur's naked upper lip
or Ernest with a smooth chin.

Today, there will be no fixed grin
no swansdown throat
no feathered hat.
I shall be as visible as a daytime bat.

Left Shoe

We hiked from Leeds to rural this,
a solid pair, and pretty.
I settled here, I wore her down,
she legged it for the city.
Now instep-sunk and upper-worn,
I'm aged from black to dirty.

My heart is cleaved like half a seg,
as light as half a twin.
All memories of sox replaced
with compost, nut husk, sin.
Only a ghost of rubber sniff,
past cobbling, my soul is thin,

O lace me, lace me up again,
I'm lost without my laces.

Learning to Love Oneself at the Age of Almost 56

'to thee the reed is as the oak,' Cymbeline IV. 2

body language in Esperanto
quizzical furrow and upturned lip
head cocked to the left as though listening
top-of-the-right-arm-of-your-glasses in your teeth

difficulties, problems, holes in a proposal
you know you will make a mountain out of this molehill
like a dog with a bone, a rat up a drainpipe
always asking the question   *what if?*

Comfort ye, comfort ye
thou art the lemming that refuses to jump over the cliff

Epitaph

I wouldn't like to be
in your shoes

You didn't choose
to end up

with regiments of poets
beating a track to your grave

as I am

past blackened stone
Octagonal Methodist Chapel

edge-to-edge slabs round
the ruined church

like lasagne
keeping it all pinned

down   No
I wouldn't want to be in your shoes

After all

you left enough clues
Yet   you are here

by the overgrown path
in an overspill cemetery

suffocating
under all those Spring flowers

On your headstone,
Hughes

Language

Swearing was banned.
Let your yeah be yeah sufficient.
And no blasphemy at any price.
Although in certain situations, when
well I never wouldn't pass muster,
Dad might allow *good lawks alive*
or maybe *lumme*, even *lumme George*
if things got really edgy. But never
blimey, blinking heck or *blast*.

These fell into the bottomless pit
of foul language, which was a sin.

I'm training the kids on the long haul
to Grandma's or other puritan kin,
not to let slip a rogue *bloody*
and definitely no *bugger* or *shit*.
'Don't fall into punctuating
every sentence with, *Oh my God*
and for Christ's sake don't mention
any form of alcohol, the lottery,
or the fact that you're gay.'

As Mum Would Have Said

*'To lose your own language was like forgetting your mother,
and as sad, in a way.'* Alexander McCall Smith

Now here's a strange thing
I think, the longer she is dead
the more I become her – not just physically
with The Bunions, Arthritic Knees,
the way I flop onto the sofa,
but in the words I speak, phrases,
intonations, accent.

These sounds keep her alive
conjure the look of her.
And she appears,
as loud as she was in life
in my kitchen,
Fancy,
I wouldn't give it house-room.

She's inhabiting my voice.
I'm even wearing my own versions
of her malapropisms,
nubile phones
reading the destructions.

The Language of Bras

My neat breasts had their own elastic.
For years, I didn't wear a bra.
And when I did,
it was fine cotton (Swedish),
that Nordic mix
of modesty and sex.

As kids on holiday we'd laughed
on the end of Bournemouth pier
at Mike Yarwood's Show
The Rawhide Bra –
'round 'em up, roll 'em in.'
Not funny now.

In Sadie's changing room,
like a hospital cubicle,
I'm trying to act dignified
as she eyes me up like a surgeon,
diagnoses a completely different size
from 'the one you've been wearing, dear',
hoists me high,.
as would an old-fashioned corsetière,
in synthetic lace and lycra
under-wired cups.

A bra that:
takes no prisoners;
snags at the touch of roughened fingers;
transforms your profile into a matron's platform;
says (as you wilt at your reflection
in the Art Shop window),

'Face it girl, your son is right,
who'd want to look at your chest,
anyway?'

Moon

As I sit in front of my real fire
rub my thumb and forefinger
along each side of my jaw
to meet in a kiss
at the point of my chin
again and again and again
like a young man
stroking his virgin beard
in contemplation,
I feel a hard hair –
a bristle, and then another.

In this as in so many other ways
I am become my mother.

I fetch my tweezers, grimace
at the mirror as I yank out
the offenders. 10 years
since the hysterectomy
and blood gush in my moon's cycle.
Bald and wild moon
you shame me in your fullness
with your smooth round face
your *O-gape*
in mock shock at my sagging neck
and tame existence.

China

Whenever you say, 'Come home, and schlep in familiar slippers,'
I feel the need to board a plane and go to China –
a place which holds no fascination, doesn't intrigue, inspire, call
                                                          to my soul –
on a form of transport I would have to be tied up or
                                                tranquillised to use.

Why, when all I desire is the comfort of your offer,
do I have an overwhelming urge to slit my throat?

The Sea Room

is calling me from beyond my means
flashing a beacon: hope/danger/hope

trawls me from dark ocean
of townscape clutter

It sings an enticing ditty

      I am a crisp room with no mildew

      Leave deep-red dusty winter
      your books
      the drone of traffic

      Bring only a pen
      some paper
      what you stand up in

      Sink into my sandy sofa
      Gaze
      out of my silent wall of windows

      Watch how the waves strive
      get nowhere
      Reflect

      Cool down
      Walk barefoot my bleached floorboards
      Take a year, stop eating

      Then sit at the blond table
      lick salt from your fingers

      and write.